No Object

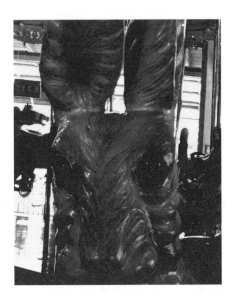

Natalie Shapero

saturnalia books

Distributed by University Press of New England
Hanover and London

Saturnalia Books
105 Woodside Rd.
Ardmore, PA 19003
info@saturnaliabooks.com

ISBN: 978-0-9833686-7-0
Library of Congress Control Number: 2012953011

Book Design by Saturnalia Books
Printing by Westcan Printing Group, Canada

Cover Art: Becky Alexander

Distributed by:
University Press of New England
1 Court Street
Lebanon, NH 03766
800-421-1561

Poems from this book were originally published in the following journals:

*Anti-, The Believer, Conduit, Dark Sky Magazine, failbetter, FENCE, FIELD, Handsome, Iron Horse
Literary Review, The Offending Adam, OH NO, Poetry Northwest, The Progressive, Redivider,
Sewanee Theological Review.*

These poems owe much to the smarts of Becky Alexander, David Baker, Jamie Boyle,
Michelle Burke, Kathy Fagan, Dave Fishman, Isabel Galbraith, Jason Gray, Andrew
Hudgins, Hilary Jacqmin, Carrie Jerrell, Matt Ladd, Tyler Meier, John Poch, Jesse Quillian,
Meg Shevenock, Cormac Slevin, Ida Stewart, Pablo Tanguay, Jen Town, Letitia Trent,
Doug Watson, and Greg Williamson.

Thanks to my family: Jonathan Shapero and Eileen Dare, Ruth Cohen and Gerald Cohen,
Adrienne Shapero, Shirlee Shapero and Marvin Shapero.

This book is for R.d.

Table of Contents

"Machines wreck themselves because some parts are weaker than others."

—Henry Ford, *My Life and Work*

Invocation: The Third and Fourth Generation of Them That Hate Me

All you need for a piano is a tree
and an elephant. I sit up sick and humming
K381, which means I am like Mozart,
having heard the music once and now
it is in me. Mozart had his harpsichord,
I have my ugly mouth. I whistle
at my plants to make them smarter.
I learn from them that Sistine
is the adjective of Sixtus. I learn from them
that Mozart was atrociously behaved,
and the pope was always angry, and the devil
was always angry, and you can't make
something flower using force, and the sins
you undertake alone will only turn you coarse.

How difficult to be a rare animal,
the pressure to stay alive. Even colors find
themselves in danger, blue eyes
that should have died out by now,
spare in their occurrence to begin with
but passed on against the odds. This can only

mean it's common to seek a blue-eyed lover.

Yes, I too have done it. I am, as the Icarus

unveiled at the wax museum, highly

lifelike. I highly like life, though in a faraway

and pent-up manner, in the way of the assassin

pining for the actress. His common

letters I have sat up reading, mouthing out

the worst of them as though

in peaceable worship of a genius teen oh DON'T

YOU MAYBE LIKE ME A LITTLE BIT? YOU MUST

ADMIT IT I AM DIFFERENT.

Stars

In the outlying laboratory they're building a star because, sure, we don't

have enough of those, we need more new things that are dead

by the time they reach us, more occupying armies in mountain towns

so remote they don't know the war is over, boys in epaulets laying a tax

on root cellars, forcing conversions to a bygone faith, yes we need more

grammar teachers repeating *left*, comma to the *left* of end quote, bracket

to the *left* and my friend said they yell that during sex, *left! oh! left*, yes

she thought everyone yelled something and I didn't know anything

better, I thought execution-style was a sex position, I thought the love line

was the biggest organ in the body, I thought you said *cock*

for one you wanted to see and *dick* for one you didn't, as in he

had a dick like a bad word I learned early, didn't comprehend the meaning,

and I don't want to live so fully, aging actress who must embody herself

dying again and again of unspecified illness, there are few good parts

for women, count your blessings, count the white like stars now shooting through my friend's black hair, she says no that's blonde, I'm a little bit

blonde, souvenir from the Hun invasion if you get my drift, yes where

were the stars while our elders were raping each other, they failed

as watchmen and now they're gone, thanks a lot, Swan, thanks a lot,

Southern Cross, I don't know why it happens, but the body is a holy

war, can't reason our way out of it, best now just to kneel.

You're Allowed

Lake I pretend is clean. Suit I pretend
is prim. Disdain this if you wish to,
you're allowed. One of the anniversaries
is wood. One of the anniversaries is clock.
Here, I made this for you, out of clock.
When do we get to wool? I will recount
the man in the hat shop who showed me his

with tab sticking out said 9 ½, that's not
my hat size, girl. Ladder into the Michigan
I cling to cold and shy, like I am tied
to railroad tracks. Be brave. You may
disdain this, but like Andy Warhol said

I DON'T PAY ANY ATTENTION TO WHAT YOU WRITE
ABOUT ME, ONLY MEASURE IT IN INCHES.

Kidding, Kidding

Ordinance says

        three coin-ops and no more.
Is this my fault? I've taken things too far.
Hard to believe I've been described as a nun

                on her day off.

Listen to me.

        You simply cannot change
the entire country to the metric system
by calling up a frog jump in La Jolla

             and pleading

they see to print

        the win in centimeters.
The frog ramp was absurdly cantilevered.

No kind of peep show parlor can survive

on fewer than

four machines.

With all the kinds of screens,
hard to believe they okayed the astronaut
who asked the tester DON'T YOU HAVE THAT INKBLOT

UPSIDE DOWN.

Though In Zero Gravity

you must learn to recognize objects standing
on any end. He bought me a drink. I said THIS PEN

CAN WRITE IN SPACE, meaning this pen
explodes on planes. A child traveling alone

was sitting between us solving a What Is Wrong.
Goldfish bowl on hot stove, kid, get

with it. Oh I am a wholly worthless person.
He said WHY IS IT THAT WE CAN'T GET OVER.

We went over it. I thought a ball
field was a radar screen. Oh I was close.

Four Fights

1.

(point) To stop a crime in progress,

        racking the action is often enough.

(counterpoint) Woody Allen: NOTHING WORTH KNOWING

CAN BE UNDERSTOOD WITH THE MIND—

    EVERYTHING REALLY VALUABLE HAS TO ENTER

YOU THROUGH A DIFFERENT OPENING.

        So much dark

I would like to be kept in. When I said you could think of me

as your therapist,

    I meant can you leave the room and I'll make notes?

2.

The housecat was declawed for her aggression, but turned only more combative post-procedure. This was against her interests and also was expected. She had developed a hypervigilant tendency, symptomatic of trauma-related stress, of being pinned and severed of defenses. She was quick to battle and couldn't fend anything off. Stitching her side at the clinic, the doctor waved away cash: COME NOW, YOUR MONEY'S NO GOOD HERE.

3.

(point) THE IT GIRL FINALLY HAD AN ORGASM AND HER DOCTOR
TOLD HER IT WAS THE WRONG KIND.

(counterpoint) Woody Allen: I'VE NEVER

          HAD THE WRONG KIND, EVER, EVER. MY WORST ONE

WAS RIGHT ON THE MONEY.

      Some girls charge by the hour; some, the act.

And what can I do for you? I'm not the healthy sky downing
a raw egg yolk at night and spitting it

              back in the morning.

    I can dish it out but can't, and how

4.

could you be so blasé

                  and how could you leave me in this low

lying state, replete with slings and swinging doors and how
many times have we all seen fucking *Manhattan*?

                  In the end, he gets with the teenage girl

and we really don't know how to feel.
                  I don't expect compassion.

Sometimes Harmful Never Helpful

We all took turns on the brakeless bike called Legs,
better a name for a gangster or his girl.

                                  I screamed

at city geese to make them scatter. Not words.
Some other shout. Then, from a car, screamed harder.
I came to hate

                  whatever I could. I came within an inch

of every inch.

                  I once did a rubbing of a man
as though he were a very important grave.

Leaving him in winter: steer, he implored, into the skid.

                            Why should I be told?
When do I not protect myself, and foremost?
Leaving him in summer, how many
times he emphasized a body is no object.

How many times I've been advised to drive into the deer.

Read It and Weep

oh please, I know no valentine

       JUST ANOTHER FRIDAY NIGHT

sour shots and pocketknives, opaque

windows, old lines

                      just take

my wife seriously

take her

the seer machine dispenses cards

       I CALL YOUR ENEMIES BY NAME

who knows if sex is prophesied

to work like water

                     you can lead

a creature but you cannot

make her

forswear the impulse magazine

       HOW I GOT MY BODY BACK

somewhere you rock your infant son

that owl face

                    everyone

assures he'll be a little heart

breaker

Examples of How To Search

1. (ANCIENT NEAR HISTORY)

The closest I have to a wedding fantasy
is this one dream of Sunday drive-up banking.
You're sending up a deposit box. The tube,
somehow kicked to a mode of extra power,
sucks off all your clothes. I am the teller
watching you drive naked across the lot,
feeling your outfit raining down on my head
and saying, sir, sir, you forgot your license.

2. (ADVENTURE AND NOT VACATION)

I go to see my lover. I sleep on the bus
as though the bus is wilderness, my coat
spread on the seat. I wake at three and reach
for a small meal I cooked in foil and burned
but couldn't bring myself to throw away.
I hear a stranger singing. Do you know
the book I'm thinking of? The regular boy

who worked as a station hand and lived in a shack
with board walls and no bath? He thought it better
to clean himself with a towel and hot tap
than end up sitting in his own old water.

3. (HAZARD! [FINDS HAZARD, HAZARDS, HAZARDOUS])

Hotel on the coast, surrounded now by bodies
of alligators. The cause of death is money
people threw in the fountain, making wishes.
The alligators ate it. I am like that,
taking into my person so many wants.
You told me once I suffered from a death wish,
and that by death you meant a lot of things.
Toss a buoy to a man overboard,
and twelve percent of the time the buoy hits
the man in the head. Tell me what to choose.

Ten Lines on a Drop Ad, or, Boys Don't Make Passes at Girls Who Wear Glasses

If you cannot see this—safari car with big

cat on the hood and woman inside who likes it—

consider a rewet. The friend who sent me said give best

to Dr. Butterface, the one who's slap-me hot

everywhere but/her/face. Dear defined lion,

I wouldn't know. I require new and darker frames,

can never find the clear ones when it's early—

they camouflage into the sill like some

adapted bug, gone pale to stay alive. I assume

this happens with any pair, it's just a matter of time.

Implausible Travel Plans

He said, the water down there, it's so clear
you can't see jellyfish. That indicates
nothing, I said, and he said, I don't care

is the hardest line to deliver in all of acting,
as though he knew of an acting laboratory
where researchers developed hardness scales

and spattered across them devastating fragments.
SHOW ME THE STEEP AND THORNY WAY TO HEAVEN.
I liked to rehearse my Ophelia during blackouts,

the traditional time to make the worst mistakes
and, later, soften the story. Nothing working
but the gas stove. God, I felt so bad

that time we used the crock instead of the kettle
and watched it smoke and shatter. I was the one.
I was the one who wanted stupid tea.

A Cup, the Amount of Blood in a Human Heart

You've grown a beard.
Stay out of dreams, or you'll mean something.
Stay close. I've kept your secrets,
haven't you heard?

You won't dispose
of sapped batteries, for fear they'll leak.
You retire them to a drawer,
where they are near

the unused ones,
and can't be told apart, and so you
are forever trying to spark
what doesn't give

a spark. Snapping
them into the kitchen clock, reading
the same wrong time of day, do
you think of me

and ever, for a little, let them stay?

I Don't Sleep in White

Religion being defined as the expectation
of future punishments, my people
sat in prayer. They sat on thatch and slashed their hair
in marriage, traveled under Gothic names
with papers sewn in the lining of their coats. I came
late, talked late, misunderstood their jokes,
those punch lines that entailed a working
comprehension of old world exchange
rates. I never prayed to God, but begged the clouds
to meet my needs: not rain, form scenes
from favored books. I was put into acting as a child,
carried by other children over the lake
of fire we were instructed to imagine. Student of ash,
I grew up fleck-complected, short of breath. I set
out seeds for small birds, watched them eat
their weight, watched others do the same. Though
I've been told white suits me, I don't sleep in white.
My bad eyes in the morning can't discern a shirt
from bedding. I am through with needing
to have such fabric handed to me, turned out
like the turned out feet of birds. Cloud, have mercy
on these small destructions. Send me to a war, I'll leave

the war. Sharpen my want of dying, I won't die.
Cloud, believe I once believed in justice.
I thought it was a bird that I could wait for: coffee
thermos, special lenses, drabbest coat at dawn.
I thought if I was quiet, I would see it. Cloud, forgive
the error. Cloud, forget the branches I have broken
in my terror. Cloud, have only patience with the lover
presenting his nakedness like the unpainted
puzzle they gave in grade school
to test if we were smart. Cloud, I was always
smart. Where has it gotten me? Haven't I
lived correctly? Haven't I fed whatever asked to be,
felt only fear of creatures whose refusal to fear me
evinced a rabidness? Why can't I be
like my grandfather, wear a heavy hat,
play Baltic anthems on the violin and just expect
that those with whom I share my life will know
how many kopeks in a ruble? My error was trusting
in acting, and sleeping in white, and building homes
for shadow birds, which means I have built homes for
many hands. There are so many kopeks in a ruble.
Cloud, there are more than you can ever know.

Orange On the Nail

Whatever is said to mate for life, doesn't. Science once was awful
at telling birds apart, took any speckled hen in the nest
for the same one every time. Now we know more.

See the shop
where the model girls are ugly. This only happens at one store,

and every time I'm there they offer me work. I say I work already,
and they say where, as though I'll soon be stolen. The fitting attendant
is angry in sandals, kicking her toes.

LOOK AT THIS COLOR, IT'S WRONG.
IT'S PEACH IN THE BOTTLE, she says. PEACH IN THE BOTTLE, ORANGE ON THE NAIL.

Is this where we've gotten to? Have I hurt you? Have I made
accusations from the other side of a stall,

put you in mind of stone
fruit grown in glass? Of seed fruit and a spike? And what about the cigarette
on the subway stairs, still going? Everyone avoids it, wishing not

to stamp it, cheering the burn as I have cheered a family animal no one
could put down. Such is our religion. We raise kids in it and cry when they sleep

with heretics. Striding neighbors

                                    beg us stay together. I can't
remember school. Once I returned to the college I'd left
and found that I knew no one.

                              I slept on the floor of a lab for making ears.
The guard woke me: HOW DID YOU GET IN? I told him I WAS A RUNNER,

THEY NEEDED A RUNNER. I TRAINED ALL SUMMER. MY EVENT WAS HURDLES.

One Hundred Degrees Is Not Twice As Cold As Fifty Degrees

Same bird out the side door for three days, is that the pain?
You can't touch a bird, it makes the other birds
reject it. You shouldn't say you are thinking
of touching a bird. You shouldn't say you have ever
heard of birds. I keep assuming it will get cold and go.

Come over. I am destroying ginger inside a glass.
Icebreaker: WHAT ONE THING IS ALL YOU HAVE?

Come over. I will tell of small helper horses bred
out of need and unable to bend at the knee, that is the trade.
To sleep, I have accepted a rigid sleep that offers no reprieve
from these unfurnished dreams. I went to school. Everything
was a test. Two cards, a rock and a cat: which is alive?

My scar I said was from folk art. This you saw through.
Woodcut: GIVE A MAN AN INCH, HE THINKS HE IS A RULER.

Come over. I will tell of your mother, how she kept birds
in the hall and taught the boy one to whistle in a sexy way.
He would do it when I walked by, even at night
when the cage was draped and he had no way of knowing
who was there. I really could have been anyone.

Bad Key

Copy of a copy, see the rut?

Nothing's born that way.
How do you think I got to be where I am today?

It shows on my face. I'm all turned down,
ill-suited to the lock of it,

the whole unluck of me.

With doors, if you can't see the hinges, it's a push.
Heavy ones you do

with both hands. Which is the way
God doesn't give.

Horse Story

This is the horse story, the story of the highway

fiend who dropped, as from a bridge, on top of me
to make, through acreage and stream,

his clean escape. A glove

burrowed in my neck. He sank his kneecap
in my flank, and we were off. I thrashed. I spoke

in whinnies, jawed the bit that was his arm. He quit

his cape. And then, the stark alarm,
the blinking of the wet woods.

How I broke, free and matted, into that lagoon

of sheriff blue. Above us hung the quartered
apple moon. The hot night clicked its tongue.

Lean Time

Without is how I go. The best defenses
fluctuate in scope and in supply.
The price of attack dogs now is very high.
I've hidden my old love's letters in a bag.
Reading one is eating from the trash.
In the dream I heard his actual laugh.

Outcasts only care what outcasts think.
I gather together the people I have hurt
and rate them. Lover's hair, like a red shirt
washed with a white shirt. Nobody can
forgive. I hate them, and they hate me back.
In the dream I heard his actual laugh.

It's often said, of eating from the trash,
that many women do it. You have slammed
the lid, but then again, it's diet be damned
and what a waste. Fries in a paper sack,
dirty from coffee grounds. I almost gagged.
In the dream I heard his actual laugh.

News To Me

Children are always last to know. The kick
and snare we'd propped up by the ironing board
heaved when our trio practiced. Sister found
bricks of cash inside the both of them,
and in our father's violin case, a gun
and eighteen rounds. Where was the violin?

The radio turned gratingly melodic.
At school, everyone missed that little teacher,
married in summer to an army man
she didn't love. The chemical salon
was doing more business than it ever had
before. I got it, then. A war was on.

Stranger

Never has it been. Never have I felt. The fashion
shifted quickly. I spent the summer switching
a specific valuable placket from blouse to blouse, pins in
my teeth at half dawn, kids already up and slumping
into tire swings. My love was an egg but he did not rot

like an egg, still hale as the outside fractured, rivet
wrinkles running down his face. He said he'd broken
a woman like an egg, or was he taking her
for the morning, was it the morning that broke, split
open and red? Something's living in there, he said

of the pin cushion tomato plucked from the bowl,
and put it back. There was a way to crack an egg and then
there was a way that eggs got cracked. Sure, a stranger
pitched me like an egg against the home
of a hated leader. And so what? I met no god. It was a time

when everyone was bleating SHOP YOUR CLOSET,
meaning we weren't wearing all we could. Take another
look, you never know. A few of us trundled around
in the cop car searching. I was in my projects,
head to toe. The cop said WILD SHIRT and I said I MADE IT.

Little Winter

1.

Just when I was finally feeling guilty
about my health, the weather turned. Too cold

to bike to the hospital, chain up and be shocked
at the good grace of it, never exactly

considering yes
of course I too am sick, why else

am I always here, inhibitor
scripts in season, piling up like so much

2.

snow. The hospital's revolving door:
synecdoche, affront.
I've walked in there with thieves and with

officials. One time with a resident
I'd slept with. He had turned me over fast

like I was burning in a pan. I hate to hug
in reunion, and so I feigned some croup,

employed the double

                    speak of DON'T TOUCH

ME—I DON'T WANT TO GIVE YOU ANYTHING.
Bad tangle. He was a robbery
gone wrong. I made off with little and so much

3.
I never said, like, baby, I don't need you
to make me hate myself—I get enough
of that at home.

                         I live alone.
Two rooms and a table. I used to say a Hail Mary

every time I heard a siren, but since moving
to this murder city I've learned

a person can only take her own praying so much.

Nominal Ordinal Interval Ratio

About that metric America: I mean it.

It's easy and it's cheap. We keep
professional foot races as they are.

We keep film cameras, still

cameras, keep the ban
on careful men who never

junk anything, as they will always

save the photos. What can I say,
I was young. What can I say,

a way to describe

my continuing face is the phrase
bad skin. I could sleep anywhere

if I ever slept. I could go on.

He drove away with a tea drink,

quilt on his stuff so thieves

could not be sure. I went on

to discover the most industrious
mouse patrolling the walls.

A friend said that is many

mice, how could you think each time
it was the same one. We keep money

as well, that is a big one.

Thomas Jefferson pushed
for decimal coinage, how it would be

easier to manage, although

in truth he was very bad that way.
He often said BUT THE DEAD,

THEY HAVE NO RIGHTS.

Our War

My town was a Quaker town with a meetinghouse
and a Quaker college, but no public school.
They bussed us down the road about ten miles.
It was all right. We drummed up friends. We dreamed
of the same stock careers, and sometimes when
we tired of talking fantasy and pop,
the locker gossip turned to threats of war.
What if our two towns fought each other? Who
would win? The answer wasn't obvious.
Some parents in the other town had guns,
but only for deer. Did that mean the deer
would take our side? Kids in the other town
were tougher, too, excelled at climbing rope
and wrestled for dollars in the parking lot.
But we had the professors. We had labs
and physicists and million dollar grants.
We could build extraordinary bombs.
We wouldn't, though. We were a peaceful town.
Show us a war, we'd say, and we'll show you
dust on the beakers. Dust on the hazard suits.

A fine thing to tell ourselves, beside the clock

and coffee shop, the Adirondack chairs.

In truth, we'd strew their fingers everywhere.

We would take their boys for infantry.

We would take their girls for making more.

Spare Me

thin displays of self-rely, cake
you've learned to make over

an open fire, lock

you're picking over an open
fire, fire you're starting

over an open fire.

The sheep ate everything
off the drying line. I had to lie

about the sweaters

so as not to call a creature
a cannibal, acrylic all,

I swear it. Why

do farm boys bring their sheep

to the edges of cliffs?

It's the only way

to make the sheep
push back. I took a while

to get that one.

I took a while to send myself
so far there were no phones

to wait by. I fell silent.
Sheep are easiest to clone

because they are natural

followers. In wartime,
so the gardeners could enlist,

Woodrow Wilson grazed

a dozen sheep on the White
House lawn. It worked out fine.

The meek, the Earth,

assess the signs. I'm living
off crab apple scraps. They said

I was too quickly

hurt. Believe me, I have
been called worse.

Arranged Hours

The low moon rattled me. Sobered, through with the good life, it arrived

papery and urgent as Marley, the ghost in the chains, the ghost always

omitted in the wrong answer three to the question HOW MANY GHOSTS

APPEAR IN A CHRISTMAS CAROL? A thin book, ratty blanket of a sort that,

when I held it, chilled me as the drafty anterooms of the starving

or haunted. It is unbefitting to believe in ghosts, to believe what one reads,

what one writes. With a vegetable knife, I excised my long-gone love

from a sheet of photographs, but I couldn't remove the shadow

he'd cast without doing violence to others. I packed my albums and drove

back to Chicago; in my absence, it had snowed incorrigibly, and I returned

to my city as though to a burgled home, the streets upended, piles of weather

and trash everywhere and the cars strewn in odd spots, no use to anyone. I am

not particularly interested in living bent on vengeance, the murder

victim who spends her last moments scrawling in sand the name of the sap

who killed her. I heard an accomplished scientist refer to the practice of autopsy
as questioning with the knife. He kissed me in a library

for special books that had no dedications. That is the idiom
of my generation. I can't speak for anyone else. I wax ever sharper,

harsher, or unchanged, I cannot say. Am I seeing things? How does
one decide who should be hurt? That moon, it was so low it was the Earth.

Hostile Platitudes

The walk-through model of the working heart
will scare you– stay away. It is most honest

to speak in truisms if you also think
in truisms, though if you dream in them,

to speak becomes dishonest once again.
Because a stranger drinking and watching you sing

will likely pity you, it is wise to request
a karaoke number full of sex

and kick. A heartsick plaint: a sorry scene.
If I've learned anything, I must be certain

nobody cares for folk tales. All they like
are hostile platitudes. Nobody wants

a history lesson, especially not now.
In ancient Rome, a prisoner brought to death

could be released if he met a vestal virgin

en route to execution. Had to be

by chance. The guys get hot for anyone

who shows up like she didn't plan to come.

No Please After You

Couldn't keep anything down. Slept in my dress.
Craned to the difficult like a fern to the sun.
Visited home and woke to my family yelling
about a neighbor who went to a funeral
and had to call it vacation for HR.
What is the world, they said. I said I agree.

My family taught me to be extremely polite,
to always pause for questions. Made my stories
interminable. The funeral was a friend,
shot in a crab shack by the man whose wife
he was screwing. Can't please everyone,
I always say, then try to. A long ago

boyfriend told me I could find success
in porn, not that I have a dynamo body
or anything, but because I am like a child,
and a high percentage of men are attracted to kids,
more than you would think. We were together
for a long time. I've never looked much older.

HOT (NORMAL)

His eyes: the Earth from space,
blue with something

in the way. Somehow
he looked womanish in the military

issue coat with chevron patch
and slashed-up underside.

WHICH ONE OF YOU IS GOING TO BE THE WIFE?

License plate: RCDVSM. Recall the servant
in Anna Karenina, watching city visitors try their hands

at making jam. She wanted them to need
her, and so prayed

it wouldn't clot. News insists the amount of old
people who are extremely old

is up. How far? The ex dragged me in nothing
but an overlarge shirt across the carpet floor, rug burns

on my backside. Splotch means an animal's impure.
In the accent he added a middle syllable, said SECRET

as though CIGARETTE.

Recidivism, really? I wanted to shoot

the cigarette out of your mouth, but you'd switched
to the patch, so I shot you in the arm.
I attended period plays in period costume,

sneaking on stage, toddling my way through the waltzes.
You said I look most naked when I'm dancing,
covering what is covered anyhow. Nothing

anyone hasn't already seen. I wanted
to shoot the secret out of your mouth.

Scene: today one billion people

live in a country other than that
of their birth. As with camping,

I leave nothing behind.
Move to the prairie, jut up

a home, spoil the quiet you seek.
Lincoln to Harriet Beecher Stowe:

AHA, SO YOU'RE THE LITTLE LADY

WHO STARTED THE BIG WAR, as though
she were Helen of Troy. Orphan Annie
to the audience, singing of invented

parents, sophisticates collecting
ashtrays and/or art.

The former's fine by me.
I've no desire
to look a horse in its whatever.

If you look straight
at a horse, you go blind.

Or do they have blinders,
is that it? What I'm thinking?
The rookie cop removes his hat,
doesn't see the thugs

laying bribes inside. He replaces
it. Bills all down his face.

Clothes machine: how it strove to instruct.
The cycle called HOT (NORMAL), like

good luck. It's said for every pretty girl,
there's a man who's sick of screwing her.
Recall how much you wanted me

to feign forgetting your day, only to know
inside. So you could be surprised.

Recall you were so tired
then, tired of the yard-bound idiot crocus
rousing in a lull between snows.

As for the sheets we slept in, I have washed
them on I think you know what rinse.

A diver comes across a sunken ship.

What he doesn't want is most

of it, the dark and rank,

the frame in which is stitched EVEN A DOG

CAN TELL IF IT IS BEING STUMBLED ON

OR BEING KICKED. Close your iron

mind to this as if

a steamer trunk you sit on top of when

it will not hitch.

A clearing is just a giving

in, forest hitting the floor to show defeat.
The gods put signs in the sky. We raze the trees for a better
view. I'm destroying my body

in hopes of same. Love, I've got this troubled
root, and I've been choked awhile,

and now I can't take cotton in my mouth.
It says in my chart cotton
is not allowed. It says in my chart some pain

here and here, and always patient considers, when pinned
under the lead shield, sex

for the first time. Always patient considers, spitting froth
into a basin, acts to remain unnamed.
My chart has a line for age at first pre-bite wing inquiry

by sylph hygienist: IS THERE ANY
CHANCE YOU MIGHT BE PREGNANT, parasols repeating

clean across her scrubs.

Sick on a weekday, sleeping under the desk
of the world while it's at work. I ask it

what it does. It doesn't answer.
It says it's on the phone. I check and find
the lines are lit.

It gives me a little job
all my own: to remind it of small things.
Buy clothing soap. Your brights:

important to keep them
bright. Important to write a one-word list

in a low-grade hand on work scrap, crayon marked BOLD.

I took a class on the Holocaust in college.
On the transcript, it showed up

as LIT OF HOLCST. I got an Incomplete.
I was in love with the man who came to sign
for deaf students. He never missed

a session. He taught me how to say I AM NOT
JEWISH. It hasn't proven useful.

When I called it quits, he took things fine.

Like a parent, said to me ALL I WANT
IS FOR YOU TO BE HAPPY. Like a parent,
what he really meant was ALL I WANT

IS FOR YOU TO BE MORE LIKE OTHER KIDS.

I haven't been a child in a long time.

At most, I've been a cat. The world has left

something on for me while it's at work.

Cats can't see TV. Or is it mirrors? I've seen a lot

of both. I've tacked toward shame.

I've read of the sham obscenity

trial of Howl, publishers in holding cells,

something in the food so they couldn't get hard.

We're lucky, our freedom. Recall

when the condom tore. I accused you

of wishing it, trying to make me settle down.

You responded SETTLE DOWN.

The folder called Trade Secrets I read

as command, responding I WILL NOT. Which is
the best part of the secret,
the keeping or the telling? I need to know. I am leaving

and only one will fit. Better to pack light
than heat, hey now. No implement

of self-defense exists
that can't be used against you.

Even the convex mirror in the trestle,
installed to show if someone lurks beyond
the station wall—even the mirror, that was how they got me.
They printed backwards books on all my clothes.

I couldn't move. I stared at myself for hours.

I think I'll tell my daughters God made breasts

by stubbing out His candy cigarettes
where the nipples now are. I saw you do that
with the real things against street signs,

saw you strike a match on the zip

fly of your pants. Trampled the rice paper grass in the row
home yard like a blaze but did not catch.

Are married people happier

or are happier people married?
Though of course who wants to adore, who could
adore, sure, and stand

with this world, the ways it takes us
all and always, burns and failing
systems and a kind of truck
they don't make anymore.

Somewhere in the funeral I realized my dress had pockets.

Little niece was craning DID HE DIE YET?
and we all tried to quiet her, though who cares, it was
anyhow just us.

Don't cry. Men could once be broken
on the wheel for peddling cottons

dyed impertinent colors. Thomas Paine:
GOVERNMENT, LIKE DRESS, IS THE BADGE

OF LOST INNOCENCE. Hey now. How far
we've come. I pull on stockings. Cloud

my eyes. Mascara. Watch the rain.
This season, like a woman: everything runs.

Flags and Axes

Maybe because I taste the dirt and am disquieted
by all I eat, knowing it came up through the earth
feeding on trash and watered by murderous
torrents, knowing its hardness by how it survived
to blossom on unstable plates that grind and slough,
like dead skin from a snake, whole houses
from their beams. Maybe because sex is a closed set
of eerie scenes, the senselessness of being eyed
and sidled through as a wall is by a ghost.
Maybe this is why I've never known
any nature but the ruthlessness with which I stay
upright. How I have killed to live and live
like this, unwell, unwelcome and unmoored and still
I have killed for it and would again. Once in a hall
built on a burned park where nothing grew,
I watched a staging of Macbeth. A child
was derided as an egg, and then they took his life,
and from my seat in the sloped corner, I saw the actual
boy was hurt in the stunt. I shrank away.
I never touch the blood of others. Only after the room
flashed on and the stage was cleared of flags and axes

did I approach. I stopped at the small ditch
where the orchestra sits when music is required.
Several stragglers were there. A rope hung on posts
across the top, and we all stood clutching it
like schoolchildren together holding a python.
Later, at a trestle shut for repair, I thought of the heft
of the rope in my hands and how I could
slip under. I wanted none of it, and nothing other.

Admonishment

Hilly here, the land an animal thrashing against the cage
of the interstate. The god I answer to is different
from the god I started with—still, I wouldn't say I get
around. What now for the newsprint newlywed,

returned from an ancient place with zero
stories: EVERY DAY ANOTHER CHANCE NOT TO DRIVE TO RUINS,

AM I RIGHT? I couldn't say. I looked away
when they pastured the steeper planes beyond the town.
As though for a portrait, sat for years
of lessons on infection and reproach for cryptic notes. It's amazing

how much you can't get from kissing.

You Call This Composition

Get me as if I'm going in I said I was standing so far back

                        on the lake beach I was almost in

the highway

           Becky snapping the sand castle close

to make me small that's a trick

              from old Hollywood but where were we surely

                 I transgress

                     surely I have said too much

        while wearing not enough but I do not request

     acceptance, only a little space

how I did plead for one more week in this city of revolving

    doors he said no he didn't trust the buses he reminded me who was it

             reported trains in Europe churn

in 4/4 time and Asian trains 3/7

his true struggle with the city

was that center always screening like rope

trick films or something and how we have nothing of nature here though what

I said about shadows

don't they count

I knew the films he meant

the lasso burning around the showgirl's waist

how in the photo spread of her at home the husband stares like stop fucking

taking our picture

The English End

Come to me now and I will, as the house
where Rilke wrote the Duino Elegies,
give you a place to sleep and make you sad.

I have done this more than was expected.

I have inhabited myself for years
like some old Gothic castle left in my care.
My heart, a bust I steadied myself against.
A bookcase spun. More than I knew was there.
If I love you,

                 know you are also loved
by all the whisper rooms I've lived with, long
and unaware. Know it, please,

                              in German.
Their word for change sounds like the English END.
I thought the Archaic Torso of Apollo
was instructing YOU MUST END YOUR LIFE.

My Life and Work

It's old cars that anger me most, slender wheels and the wheezing,

engines screwed by broken men with drop cloths spread

over hospital beds—Ford said they were happy to do it,

and so they were. How can these boxes keep on, year after year

at the Blues and Something Fair, unrelenting in their wrongness,

oblivious to progress? It has gotten so I'm afraid

to step even into the street, old cars aligned and beeping

outside the ballet school where once I saw so many children

dart from underneath the skirt of Mother Ginger in a bad

Nutcracker Suite. I felt then my own sickness:

sudden and antique. How I was held in real restraints

as the sweet plums danced on plates and the tin toys came to life.

Close Space

Because I am good at crying
alone I watch my cousins' kids
when there's a funeral. Spare
the pamphlets, prayer and cakes—
it's better on my own.
The kids find sleep and then I watch
the phone, with its rich history
of shrill communiqués, one mean
love's shame, another one's rebuke
to never call and what is it
they say of whores? You pay
them not for how they screw you
but for how they go away.
I so want to be a sweetheart,
but I've never been able to stop
the raw needling, haymaking,
futile and forever by pain
belied, as when I saw them
suited and starched: WHO DIED?

This is America. Let me be
sick of close space, shooting for
bodies off and unknown.
Let me say loudly: from the next
exploration, men will not return.
It must be just that far. It must
be just that steep, bad shore
of star where a theorist strangles
vicious things for meals,
then dies for theory and is burned.
He wouldn't be the first.
I know well the story of the noble
dispatched for life to terrorize
an island. He asked of his king
only to guarantee there would be
women. Would I were there
to answer: DEAR DUMB BUCK,
REQUEST WAS FILED UNDER YOU WISH
FOR, BE CAREFUL WHAT.

Attributions

John Hinckley, Jr., Letter to Jodie Foster: "Don't you maybe like me a little bit? (You must admit it I am different.)"

Tom Wolfe, *The Right Stuff*: "[Pete] Conrad stares at the piece of paper and then looks up at the man and says in a wary tone, as if he fears a trick: 'But it's upside down.'"

Roald Dahl, *Danny the Champion of the World*: "When I needed a bath, my father would heat a kettle of water and pour it into a basin. Then he would strip me naked and scrub me all over, standing up. This, I think, got me just as clean as if I were washed in a bathtub—probably cleaner because I didn't finish up sitting in my own dirty water."

Shakespeare, *Hamlet*, Act I, Scene 3: "Show me the steep and thorny way to Heaven."

Tracy Egan Morrisey, "BINge Eating: When You Eat the Garbage You've Tried To Throw Out": "I went over to the garbage, found the other half of my sandwich and ate it, despite the fact that an empty packet of wet dog food was right next to it."

Daniel T. Kobil, "The Quality of Mercy Strained: Wresting the Pardoning Power From the King": "[T]he Romans introduced an element of chance into the clemency process by automatically pardoning criminals sentenced to death if they encountered a Vestal Virgin on the way to the place of execution, so long as the encounter was an accidental one."

Thomas Jefferson, Letter to Samuel Kercheval: "But the dead have no rights."

Leo Tolstoy, *Anna Karenina*: "Agafya Mikhailovna, her face flushed and angry, her hair untidy and her thin arms bare to the elbows, was moving the preserving pan over the brazier with a circular motion, looking darkly at the raspberries and devoutly hoping they would stick together and not cook properly."

Charles Strouse and Martin Charnin, "Maybe": "Betcha they're young / Betcha they're smart / Bet they collect things / Like ashtrays and art."

Oliver Wendell Holmes, *The Common Law*: "Even a dog knows the difference between being stumbled over and being kicked."

Shigeyoshi Murao, *Footnotes To My Arrest For Selling Howl*: "For lunch they served me wieners, very red. The trusty told me that the sausages were full of salt-peter so that the prisoners would not get hard-ons."

Shakespeare, *Macbeth*, Act IV, Scene 2: "What, you egg!"

Blaise Cendrars, "The Prose of the Trans-Siberian": "European trains are in 4/4 while the Asian ones are in 5/4 or 7/4."

Henry Ford, *My Life and Work*: "We have experimented with bedridden men—men who were able to sit up. We put black oilcloth covers or aprons over the bed and set the men to work screwing nuts on small bolts."

Also Available from saturnalia books:

Nowhere Fast by William Kulik

Arco Iris by Sarah Vap

The Girls of Peculiar by Catherine Pierce

Xing by Debora Kuan

Other Romes by Derek Mong

Faulkner's Rosary by Sarah Vap

Gurlesque: the new grrly, grotesque, burlesque poetics edited by Lara Glenum and
Arielle Greenberg

Tsim Tsum by Sabrina Orah Mark

Hush Sessions by Kristi Maxwell

Days of Unwilling by Cal Bedient

Letters to Poets: Conversations about Poetics, Politics, and Community
edited by Jennifer Firestone and Dana Teen Lomax

Artist/Poet Collaboration Series:

Velleity's Shade by Star Black / Artwork by Bill Knott
Polytheogamy by Timothy Liu / Artwork by Greg Drasler
Midnights by Jane Miller / Artwork by Beverly Pepper
Stigmata Errata Etcetera by Bill Knott / Artwork by Star Black
Ing Grish by John Yau / Artwork by Thomas Nozkowski
Blackboards by Tomaz Salamun / Artwork by Metka Krasovec

Winners of the Saturnalia Books Poetry Prize:

Lullaby (with Exit Sign) by Hadara Bar-Nadav
My Scarlet Ways by Tanya Larkin
The Little Office of the Immaculate Conception by Martha Silano
Personification by Margaret Ronda
To the Bone by Sebastian Agudelo
Famous Last Words by Catherine Pierce
Dummy Fire by Sarah Vap
Correspondence by Kathleen Graber
The Babies by Sabrina Orah Mark

No Object was printed using the font Avenir Roman.

www.saturnaliabooks.org